Lord Baltimore

English Politician and Colonist

Colonial Leaders

Lord Baltimore *English Politician and Colonist*

Benjamin Banneker *American Mathematician and Astronomer*

William Bradford *Governor of Plymouth Colony*

Benjamin Franklin *American Statesman, Scientist, and Writer*

Anne Hutchinson *Religious Leader*

Cotton Mather *Author, Clergyman, and Scholar*

William Penn *Founder of Democracy*

John Smith *English Explorer and Colonist*

Miles Standish *Plymouth Colony Leader*

Peter Stuyvesant *Dutch Military Leader*

Revolutionary War Leaders

Benedict Arnold *Traitor to the Cause*

Nathan Hale *Revolutionary Hero*

Alexander Hamilton *First U.S. Secretary of the Treasury*

Patrick Henry *American Statesman and Speaker*

Thomas Jefferson *Author of the Declaration of Independence*

John Paul Jones *Father of the U.S. Navy*

Thomas Paine *Political Writer*

Paul Revere *American Patriot*

Betsy Ross *American Patriot*

George Washington *First U.S. President*

Colonial Leaders

Lord Baltimore

English Politician and Colonist

Loree Lough

Arthur M. Schlesinger, jr.
Senior Consulting Editor

Chelsea House Publishers

Philadelphia

Produced by Robert Gerson Publisher's Services, Avondale, PA

CHELSEA HOUSE PUBLISHERS
Editor in Chief Stephen Reginald
Production Manager Pamela Loos
Director of Photography Judy L. Hasday
Art Director Sara Davis
Managing Editor James D. Gallagher

Staff for *LORD BALTIMORE*
Project Editor Anne Hill
Project Editor/Publishing Coordinator Jim McAvoy
Contributing Editor Amy Handy
Associate Art Director Takeshi Takahashi
Series Design Keith Trego

The Chelsea House World Wide Web address is http://www.chelseahouse.com

First Printing
1 3 5 7 9 8 6 4 2

Library of Congress Cataloging-in-Publication Data

Lough, Loree.
Lord Baltimore / by Loree Lough.
   p.   cm. — (Colonial Leaders)
Summary: A biography of the Catholic baron who became the founder
of the state of Maryland.
ISBN 0-7910-5349-0 (hc); ISBN 0-7910-5692-9 (pb)
1. Baltimore, George Calvert, Baron, 1580?–1632 Juvenile literature.
2. Colonial administrators—Maryland Biography Juvenile literature.
3. Maryland—History—Colonial period, ca. 1600–1775 Juvenile literature.
[1. Baltimore, George Calvert, Baron, 1580?–1632.   2. Colonial administrators.
3. Maryland—History—Colonial period, ca. 1600–1775.]   I. Title. II. Series.
F184.C13L68   1999
975.2'02092—dc21
[B]   99-33136
                                            CIP

Publisher's Note: In Colonial and Revolutionary War America, there were no standard rules for spelling, punctuation, capitalization, or grammar. Some of the quotations that appear in the Colonial Leaders and Revolutionary War Leaders series come from original documents and letters written during this time in history. Original quotations reflect writing inconsistencies of the period.

Contents

Yorkshire County, located in northern England, is still a land of rolling green hills and spacious farms, as it has been for many generations. George Calvert's ancestry apparently included several farmers and landowners.

The Calvert Background

The first **baron** of Baltimore, George Calvert, was the founder of Maryland, one of the original 13 colonies.

George was born in Kipling, North Yorkshire County, England, in about 1580. No one is sure of the exact date. George's early history is made up of many scattered pieces and vague details rather than a careful collection of facts. This is partly due to the problems of the times. Records were often burned by the Crown to maintain control of the royal subjects, particularly if it was suspected the subjects were Roman Catholics. And George's parents were both Roman Catholics.

Historians *do* know that George was the eldest son of Alicia de Crossland (some records list her name as Grace) and Leonard Calvert, a gentleman from Yorkshire, England. George's father was a successful landowner who was also involved in the beef trades. In the early 1600s people often took their last names from what they did for a living, and the name Calvert may come from "calf herd."

Alicia, the daughter of John Crossland of West Riding, was an heiress in her own right. Since she had no brothers, she inherited her father's entire estate. These holdings became the property of Leonard Calvert after her death. Leonard married a second time, and nothing more is known of George Calvert's mother or her family.

The Calverts had been a well-known family in Yorkshire for generations. One branch of the family came from a Flemish background and were weavers who migrated to Yorkshire when the county became famous for growing wool.

George's father was a prosperous landowner involved in cattle farming, and the family name may be derived from that business.

Some records say that the Calverts of Yorkshire were tenant farmers and yeomen, and that in addition to leaving land, homes, and farm animals to their heirs, the Calverts of these days put aside a lot of money to pay for a good education for their sons.

George's parents were probably not very well educated themselves. Like most families, the Calverts were expected to **tithe** their estate to the country's official church, the Church of England. The required tithe was 10 percent, but the Calverts gave more, which the royal family would have seen as a sign of devotion to the queen. Therefore they would have allowed the Calverts to take advantage of one the few ways in which parents of that time could provide a future of social acceptance and financial success for their sons.

When George was born, Elizabeth I was the queen of England. Because Catholics were persecuted in those days, George's father decided that it would be best for his family to

Queen Elizabeth I was England's ruler when George was born. The Church of England was founded by Elizabeth's father, Henry VIII, and everyone was expected to belong to the country's official religion.

change religions, and so they became Anglicans.

George's father did not follow English rule willingly, however. Leonard and Alicia were frequently ordered by authorities to follow Anglican practices. By 1580 Leonard had filed a certificate claiming that he had, indeed, finally obeyed the queen. Two years later, it is believed that Leonard was imprisoned for failing to worship in the Church of England.

Whether his release was granted because he paid a fine is not known, but an entry in the Yorkshire High Commission Act reads, "Leonard Calvert of Kipling, gentleman, and his wife, appeared before the High Commission. Leonard took a bond declaring that he would have no Catholic servants, nor would he hire a Catholic teacher to tutor his children. He promised to purchase, within one month's time, a Book of Common Prayer, a Bible in English, and a catechism, which would lie open in his house 'for everyone to read.'" His children were to be put into schools in York and were not to leave without permission from the **Archbishop** of York.

Two of the children—George and Christopher, then 10 and 12 years of age—were to "learn with Mr. Fowberry at Bilton." Additionally, the boys were scheduled to appear before the commissioners once every quarter to "see how they perfect in learning."

Meanwhile, Jesuit missionaries who had slipped into England around the year of George's birth began spreading English Catholicism far and wide. These men were no doubt greatly disappointed by the number of Catholics who decided to exchange Catholicism for the Anglican Church. Still, they were sympathetic with the Catholics' plight, for the choice to remain Catholic could be very dangerous.

Catholics were not allowed to carry weapons or keep them in their homes. Their travel in and out of England was severely restricted. They were required to attend Anglican services, and were warned against holding services of their

Catholics had to wait for acceptance before they could build grand churches. While an established and widely practiced religion today, in George Calvert's time Catholicism was a fine punishable by jail time and even death.

own. Their children were to be educated as Anglicans. Indeed, without an Anglican education, Catholics would be prevented from obtaining work in most professions. Furthermore, no Catholic could hold public office.

Catholics were routinely fined a lot of money for practicing their faith. If a man was proven by the Crown to be a Catholic, he could be branded a traitor or convicted of **treason**. And to be discovered a priest was an offense punishable by death.

Despite all of this, a quiet, underground kind of war was being fought in secret places around England. The Jesuit priests wanted to do more than merely keep Catholicism up and running– they wanted to strengthen it.

These Elizabethan Catholics, while they remained the minority, would one day play an important role in young George Calvert's life.

George was extremely proud of his homeland of Yorkshire, with its beautiful fields
and valleys that were dotted with streams
and old stone walls.

2

George Calvert's Early Years

The home where George grew up showed him the benefits of honest work. His parents taught him and his siblings that hard work and a good education was the formula for success. George took them at their word, and made the best of the limited schooling that was available to him.

He felt a great loyalty to his homeland and would later write in a letter to his friend Sir Thomas Wentworth, "I love Richmondshire with all my heart, and it warms me when you talk of it, even as cold a country as it is!"

Richmond was indeed a lovely place for a boy to grow up. In George's mind it was far better than other villages of its kind. And what boy wouldn't be proud of his hometown, when in the distance he could see a great, ruined castle high on a cliff overlooking a river. Yorkshire was a region made up of many plateaus, some that rose 2,500 feet into the sky. The rock-strewn valleys were divided here and there by fast-moving streams that emptied into wild, green glens before flowing into open country.

In George's era, childhood was pretty much over by the age of 10 or 12. This is not so surprising when you realize that the average life expectancy was only 35 years. This is why it was so important for a young man to take full advantage of every opportunity that presented itself.

Even at the age of 10, George worked hard in school and earned the admiration of fellow students and teachers alike. And at a time when relatively few people could read or write (even the kings and queens themselves had only a little education), learning was in and of itself quite an accomplishment. It is believed that George was quite good at reading and mathematics, but his handwriting was another matter entirely. (King Charles I would later tease George, saying, "He writ as fair a hand to look upon as any man in England . . . from afar off; but when any one came near it, they were not able to read a word."

But poor penmanship didn't hinder George Calvert—quite the contrary. He went on to earn a bachelor's degree from Trinity College at Oxford in 1597. At that time he was barely 17 years of age. By 1605 he had received a master's degree, which was a great achievement in an age and a country where opportunities for a solid education were terribly limited. Or where, on a routine basis, the king's men could snatch children from their parents if Catholicism was so much as suspected. Protestant books were the only ones that were allowed to be purchased or displayed in family homes.

When he was barely eight years old, George, like many children whose parents had exchanged their Catholic behaviors for Anglican ones, was unaware of the dangers his father's decision had saved him from. Like any boy his age, he was far more interested in the whispered conversations of adults, discussions that involved one of the most memorable events of young George's life: the destruction of the Spanish Armada.

One dark night, beacon fires lit the skies all over England, warning the citizens that the mighty Armada was about to invade. The knowledge that war was close at hand must have caused the boy great anguish and fear. He didn't have to be a grown-up to understand that despite preparations that were underway to fend off the enemy, England just might be defeated.

And then word spread through the countryside that Sir Francis Drake had destroyed the enemy. Once again, George could continue his education with a mind free from worry about attack from the Spanish Armada.

George's father was by no means a rich man, but he did manage to save enough money to send

A statue in Plymouth, England, commemorates the English admiral Sir Francis Drake, best remembered for circumnavigating the earth and for his important role in defeating the Spanish Armada.

George to Trinity College at Oxford. Just as he had as a young boy, George saw many religious differences during his college years, too. The Puritans who ran the university were very strict about their interpretation of the Bible. But others did not agree with their ceremonies and rituals.

Queen Elizabeth herself said during a visit to the university in 1592 that if Oxford was to last forever, it must care first for the worship of God, not according to every man's opinions, but as the law of God and the queen required. This was the attitude of the day.

George shared a room at the university with several young men of his age group. He interviewed with the dean of Trinity, who decided

Spanish Armada was the name given to the Spanish ships that were outsmarted by the British sailors in the summer of 1588. Not only did England's triumph prevent that country from being controlled by the Spanish, it also provided the opportunity for the addition of colonies to the nations of England, Holland, and France. Sir Francis Drake (1543–1596) was one of the British ship captains responsible for successfully overtaking Spanish sailing vessels in the Caribbean and Mexico.

Spain assembled an armada of ships in the hopes of gaining control over more of the world, but the Spanish Armada proved no match for the power of the British fleet.

that George's credentials were satisfactory and entered George's name in the "Butterfly Book," where he kept track of charges for supplies such as bread, meat, and beer.

George was allowed to choose a tutor who would oversee his studies. The tutor would be responsible not only for George's lessons, but for his behavior as well. If George had no particular tutor in mind, the dean would choose one for him.

George was then required to stand before the vice chancellor for formal admission to the university, after which he was required to sign the subscription book. This was a very important act, for it involved promising to obey the Thirty-Nine Articles of the Church of England as well as the Book of Common Prayer.

George's signature, written in strong, bold letters beside the date July 12, 1594, can still be seen in the subscription book. After his name appears "pleb. fil." (standing for *plebei filius,* which means "son of **yeoman**"). This is considered quite odd,

George was a gifted student who attended
Trinity College at Oxford University, entering
at the young age of 14.

since his father had always been referred to as "gentleman" or "**armiger**." Historians have no way of knowing why it was written this way. The clerk who accepted the entrance fee could have made an error. Or George may have made the claim because the university entrance fee for a commoner was only four pence, while it cost a shilling for a gentleman. George was only 14 years of age at the time. More than likely, he was simply trying to save his father a little money.

Students from age 13 to 20 routinely entered Oxford. Still, since his elementary school performance had proven him to be a student of great promise, Oxford was an obvious choice for his formal education. Only 10 to 25 students were admitted each year, and only about half of them stayed long enough to earn degrees.

Each day began with religious services at six in the morning. Church was followed by a lecture in logic or math, after which the boys would eat breakfast while listening to more lectures in philosophy and metaphysics. Lunch (called "midday dinner") was intended for quiet contemplation. Bible readings, recited by one of the university **scholars**, were the backdrop of this hour. Next, the young men moved on to listen to still more lectures on Greek or Latin. Students hoping to earn a bachelor's degree were required to participate in debates on topics such as ethics, physics, or politics.

In order to make all this study and debate easier for its students, the university allowed the boys to use the library, where a small collection of books was housed, and each book was securely chained to its shelf. Books of any kind were considered rare treasures, and Oxford simply couldn't afford to take the chance that one of their precious volumes would disappear.

Outdoor exercise was encouraged. Plays and other such performances were promoted by the university's administrators. "Popular theater," however, was absolutely not allowed. In fact, the year before George arrived at

Oxford, the townspeople gathered to prohibit "common players" from coming within five miles of town.

There are not many records that tell of George's days at Oxford, but one piece of information is proof of his scholastic abilities. In 1596 England was shocked by the sudden death of its ambassador to France, Sir Henry Unton, a graduate of Oxford. Unton's admirers published a volume of verse in his honor, and this is what George Calvert contributed at the age of 16:

> While there was an early age for its wonders famed,
>> These the poets used to sing:
>> And grieving humans other forms assumed
>> And lost their former shape:
> Thus Phaeton's daughters, mourning their lost brother,
>> Thus Niobe, and thus unhappy Cypress.
> But if they sing the truth and ancient times return,
>> You, Unton, will remembered be;
> Now while some mourner in the urn thy ashes

Puts, and shrouds them in the tomb;
Into stone or marble he is changed, nor ever
fades
Unton's monument perpetual.

His talent for writing would be realized by many in the years to come.

In February 1597, less than three years after entering Oxford, George was presented with a bachelor's degree. He didn't come by it easily, however. George received the degree by way of special permission that allowed him to complete his studies in 13 terms, rather than the 16 generally required for graduation.

Sons of noblemen were almost automatically excused from at least four terms. But, having registered at the college as the son of a yeoman, George wasn't automatically granted this **petition**. Instead, he was required to present a special written request—*in Latin*—to the university authorities, in which he would explain his reasons for requesting the permission. Translated into English, this is what George wrote:

Dispensation for George Calvert, to enable him to propose a grace in the House of Congregation [meaning to carry his request to the body controlling the granting of degrees].

George Calvert, eldest son of a gentleman and student in the faculty of the arts at Trinity College, begs the venerable **Convocation** of doctors and masters, both regent and non-regent, that having spent 13 terms in the study of dialectic, responded twice in Lent under a bachelor, been created a general sophister and satisfied all the requirements of the new statutes, he may be allowed, with your kind dispensation, to propose a grace in the House of Congregation whereby he may be admitted to read some book of logic, notwithstanding the statute. The reason is that he is soon to leave the university, and as he has been called away by his parents to study municiple law, he thinks that this degree will confer no slight distinction on him.

George was asking if he could read a book instead of finishing the last three terms. After fulfilling his promise, he would be eligible for his bachelor's degree. What reason did George give for wanting to leave Oxford a little early?

He claimed his parents wanted him to study law.

His request was approved, and George received his degree in a simple ceremony during which the university's vice chancellor handed out diplomas in much the same way as graduates are awarded them today. In the autumn of 1597, George Calvert left Oxford, degree in hand.

King James I, who succeeded Queen
Elizabeth on the English throne,
visited Oxford in 1605 to grant
degrees to many people, including
George Calvert.

3

Formal
Education

During the 12 months following the graduation ceremony, George probably traveled
throughout Europe, a common practice for new
graduates at that time. After his holiday, according to
the Register of the Lincoln's Inn, a London law
school, George signed his name, but gave little information otherwise. The inscription names Yorkshire
as his home, "gentleman" as his status.

Life at Lincoln's Inn was severe by today's standards. Although students were given private rooms
in the old campus buildings, George and his fellow
scholars were required to eat all meals in the great
hall, which had been built in 1492. They studied

hard, listened to lectures and argued cases in law, and participated in formal debates. These studious young men wore caps and gowns almost every day.

But life at Lincoln's Hall wasn't all work and no play. Often the students threw huge parties, especially at holiday times. Surprisingly, there was much celebration at these parties, including dancing.

Students were required to study at least seven years to earn their law degree. George spent only three years at Lincoln's Inn, and his sudden departure from the school is not explained. It is possible that someone made him a job offer. Or perhaps the expenses associated with completing his education at Lincoln's Inn were too great for him to bear. One thing is clear: between 1601 and 1603, there is no record of how George spent his time.

By April of 1603, soon after Queen Elizabeth died, George returned from Paris with a message for Sir Robert Cecil, secretary of state. Richard

Percival, an employee of Sir Robert's, wrote to his master to welcome King James I on his trip from Edinburgh to London: "As I had ended this, my fellow George Calvert came with a pacquet from Paris, which (having taken a copy for the Lords) is sent herewithall."

This probably means that George was working for Cecil at that time. Percival's reference to George as a "fellow" indicates that he and George were both junior secretaries to Cecil, and that they also sometimes worked as clerks and **couriers**.

It is not known exactly how George was able to get a position like this at such an early age. But thanks to this job, George earned recognition at court—recognition that enabled him to progress toward high office at a very rapid pace.

It is said that on a visit to Oxford in 1605, King James and his court arrived to bestow honorary master's degrees on 43 people. The way the story goes, the king and his **retinue** were to be received on August 27, 1605, in a meadow near town. The "welcoming committee" (including the mayor and various town officials, Oxford's chancellor and vice chancellor, and other faculty heads) were to be adorned in ceremonial gowns. A conflict arose when the town officials took their places ahead of university administrators, and the lot of them were scolded soundly by the king.

Afterward, James retired to his rooms in Christ Church College, where an entire wall had been removed and pews had been taken out to enlarge his quarters, and a celebration began. Speeches, comedies, sermons, and convocations occurred in rapid succession while James argued (in Latin) with the university's best scholars on topics such as religion, tobacco, and witchcraft.

Since King James's son, Prince Henry, had been lucky enough to be born into royal heritage, Oxford was about to award Henry an honorary master's degree. But the king refused to

During his visit to Oxford, King James stayed at Christ Church College, designed by the famous architect Sir Christopher Wren.

This book collection shown here from Oxford's Bodleian Library, was gradually expanded over the years and is now one of the finest in the world.

allow it because his son was only 11 years old.

And then, finally, it was August 30: Awards Day. Those students who would receive degrees wore black gowns, faced to the hems with white taffeta, and black hoods lined with white miniver (a type of white fur). Among those getting degrees were Cecil's two young secretaries, Levinus Munck and George Calvert.

It is said that the king himself fell asleep during the speeches, plays, and sermons given that day. On one occasion, when applause roused him from a nap, James ordered that a speech be ended.

After the ceremonies, James visited the library, where the collection had grown slightly— and the books were all still chained to the shelves.

George had no trouble staying awake through the day, because he knew that the degree in his hand would take him far.

George served as secretary to Sir Robert Cecil, who was the earl of Salisbury. The Salisbury region had been one of the most important in England, and is still world-renowned for its magnificent cathedral.

4

George Calvert's Politics

Among the rumors and gossip that blur the facts of George Calvert's career come the reliable words of his cousin, Sam Calvert. In many letters to George and others, Sam complained about a lot of things, including the way the "older generation" disapproved of his beloved theater. He spent a lot of time whining about various aches and pains, but despite his imaginary sicknesses, Sam earned the respect and loyalty of many, including George. Because George and his cousin Sam were close, Sam often wrote to George, sharing many secrets. It was Sam who had introduced George to Sir Robert Cecil, the earl of Salisbury. Now, as secretary to Cecil, George had direct access to the Court.

Sam reported in a letter to a friend that in 1605 his cousin George married a woman named Anne Mynne. The marriage was most definitely not a matter of the heart, although according to Sam, affection did grow between George and Anne. In George's day, romantic love was not considered an important element for marriage. George was a practical young man, well aware of what possibilities lay in his future if he married Anne Mynne, whose family was quite wealthy.

As was the custom, the fathers of Anne Mynne and George Calvert discussed the "agreement" that would unite their two families. Afterward, since both Anne and George were already 25 (relatively old by the marrying age standards of the day), each partner began to understand that there was much to gain from this merger. George's father, Leonard, knew that in a society governed by class and connections, his son would profit from the union. Anne's father, on the other hand, realized that in a day and age when all women were considered second-class citizens, marriage to a man from a **prominent** family would assure his daughter a future that would be as prosperous as her past.

It was a sensible match. And so they were married.

The newly married George quickly became a recognizable presence in Salisbury's court. George also learned to recognize a few important things himself, such as how to cultivate the aid and assistance of the powerful men who held high office. Though George's salary was substantial, especially for one so young, he didn't enjoy the job very much, mostly because he was forced to worship God in the Anglican church when he wanted the freedom to practice Catholicism.

In 1607 Sam reported in another letter to a friend that George and Anne had purchased a house in Charing Cross. Sam said their house stood among a group of Tudors on the west side of the quaint street. Their neighbors were Sir John Stanhope, Lord Harrington, Sir Robert Naunton (who would become secretary of state), and Sir Jerome Bowes (former ambassador to Russia).

George's steady career progress inspired gossip, but he refused to let it distract him from his goals.

When the second **charter** of the Virginia Company of London received royal approval, George's name was among the 600 incorporators (including Sir Humphrey Weld, Lord Mayor of London). It was proof that George had invested his own funds in the enterprise. A few months later, he purchased shares in the East India Company as well.

George had given in to the financial adventures of the day and joined the search for wealth in the expansion of English trade.

In October 1609, when a clerk of the Signet left office, the king gave George the appointment. This was quite an amazing turn of events,

After George and Anne married, they moved
to Charing Cross. Though this modern view
of London's central area is quite different
from George's time, some of the old buildings
still remain.

considering that not too long before this, George had been criticized for not trying harder to get that very job!

Of the appointment, Sam wrote, "My cousin George Calvert hath by my Lord Cecil's private intention gotten a patent to the Signet Office!"

George's duties included drafting papers for the king's signature. This meant he would be directly under His Highness's supervision. It also meant he would have the king's ear. The new job didn't come with a raise in pay, but it put George in a position to earn the king's trust. That trust would soon come in handy.

Later that same year, a member of the Cornwall constituency died. Because the earl of Salisbury needed votes to carry out his compromise policy for increasing the king's revenues, he asked that the mayor of Bossiney let him choose the man's replacement. It was no surprise that Salisbury appointed George Calvert to the position.

George joined Parliament when it opened in

February 1610. As a new member, he felt unsure of himself, especially in the presence of older and more experienced supporters of the king.

But during the session, one of the clerks of the Privy Council fell ill, and George was chosen to take his place. A short time later he took an oath to begin working at this important job.

Many benefits came with the appointment. For one, George was now in a position to have daily conference with ministers of state–and with the king himself.

"My cousin George," wrote Sam, "was last Sunday sworn Clerk of the Council in ordinary with great grace and favor."

George was finally able to resign from Sir Robert Cecil's service.

Sir George Calvert Lord Baltimore.

Once George Calvert's political career began, his progress was swift and steady— so swift, in fact, that he delayed taking on a royal appointment for which he felt unprepared.

Rise to
the Top

S oon after the death of an elderly clerk of the
council, George found himself appointed to
fill yet another empty post. George, along with
Clement Edmondes, a fellow clerk of the council,
were to share the job. No sooner had George grown
accustomed to his new title than he was sent abroad.

And Sam wrote to his friend Trumbull, "It will
seem strange to you my worthy cousin George
Calvert should so soon upon his admission to the
Council Chamber with so much grace as never any
better, go abroad, not to see you only which he
resolved on ere he returned but all the Low Coun-
tries, beginning by Zeeland and Holland, takes the

army in his way, and so to Paris if his curiosity lead him not aloof to Strasbourg, etc., according to his direction . . . now he is gone, I must live in ignorance for ought I can learn at Court."

By now, George and Anne were the proud parents of four children. His frequent business trips on behalf of the king made life hard for his wife, who was forced to raise the children without her husband's help. Anne was not a strong woman and she was often sick. Of this, Sam wrote, "I pray God send him health and comfort, for his wife is ill. She hath so long languished upon a lingering sickness. I protest unto you there are not many such friends living, nor many such women, such is the love she hath gained amongst her husband's kindred . . . I shall miss her."

But Anne recovered and gave birth to seven more children, all of whom were baptized according to the Anglican religion. Not only did she disprove Sam's gloomy prediction, but she outlived him, too.

In 1619 the king wanted to name George one of his principal secretaries of state. But George disqualified himself, stating he was not ready to fill the shoes of his old master, Sir Robert Cecil.

George became Lord Baltimore in 1625, and Maryland's largest city was later named after him. The city of Baltimore, pictured here in colonial times, went on to become a busy port and business center.

6

George Calvert and the Colonies

Thanks to his formal education—especially his knowledge of foreign languages—George could be in constant and close contact with the king. James saw himself as the champion of Protestantism, not only in Britain, but throughout Europe, and he tried to answer the disturbing pronouncements of the Dutch **theologian** Conrad Vorstius, who questioned the body of accepted Christian teachings and divine omnipotence.

James called on George to assist him in writing a very strong answer. In French, James demanded that the Dutch expel Vorstius from his post (this was eventually done), and included in his letter of correspondence with the States General of Holland.

Here was George's golden opportunity!

Something of a scholar himself, George had already earned a place in the king's esteem. How much of the letter was written by James and how much was penned by George, no one can say for sure. But the quiet, witty sense of humor balanced by violent expressions used in that letter have been compared to other letters written by George. In any event, the king most definitely approved of George's contributions to the correspondence. Because he approved, he rewarded him by sharing even more of his private thoughts and concerns with George Calvert, James's newest secretary of state.

George had earned a reputation for being an intelligent, devoted official. Unfortunately, the reputation made him a prime choice for difficult assignments, the type James referred to as "prickly." George accepted each assignment willingly, because he had a plan.

One of George's assignments was to search

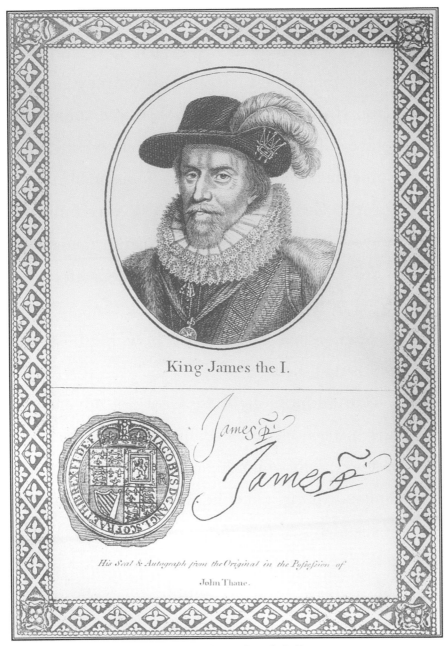

King James the I.

His Seal & Autograph from the Original in the Possession of

John Thane.

King James called on his faithful supporter George for help in many areas. He eventually made Calvert secretary of state.

for incriminating evidence in the private quarters of several gentlemen, such as Christopher Darcy, Sir Francis Bacon, and Attorney General Hobart. George was then asked to examine the offices of John Cotton, a Catholic whom King James believed had written a "treasonable tract." In 1613 George was appointed to a commission to investigate the charges brought against the Lord Deputy by Catholic members of Parliament of Ireland. Though nothing came of these probes, James appreciated how hard George worked at them.

Furthermore (and to George's advantage), the inspections allowed him to visit Ireland, a country with which his name would be forever linked. All the while, he was busy increasing his investments in the East India Company. Profits earned by the cargoes arriving from the Far East were stirring the curiosity—and the greed—of those with extra cash to spend.

This fact did far more than raise the bank balances of the company's investors; George's

One of the "prickly" assignments James gave to George was an investigation into the background of certain gentlemen, including Sir Francis Bacon.

financial knowledge awakened a whole new round of gossip-mongering. But the rumors did not affect George's reputation because a month later, he was defended by friends in high places, and sent on yet another kingly errand to seek out traitors.

James's assignments were directly responsible for George's next bold move. He was now ready to ask for a few favors. It is believed he drafted an eloquent letter dated December 3, 1614:

> To the King's Most Excellent Majesty, the humble petition of George Calvert, Your Majesty's servant.
>
> Who having many times received sundry testimonies of your Majesty's most gracious favor to his exceeding comfort, doth now in assurance thereof presume to be an humble suitor unto your Majesty for reversion of the office of Master of the Rolls in Ireland, which if your majesty shall vouchsafe to bestow upon him shall in all dutiful thankfulness acknowledge your Majesty's singular goodness toward him in that, as in many things else, for which, as he is infinitely bound he doth daily pray for your prosperous, long and happy reign.

Was the letter *really* written by George? The question remains unanswered, because although the penmanship is similar to George's, there are numerous irregularities in the script and the letter is unsigned.

Whatever the answer, George was by now deeply involved in all sorts of public affairs. In his personal affairs, he was prosperous. George felt it was time to take the biggest risk of his career to date.

First George bought some land in Richmondshire near the farm where he grew up. Next he claimed possession of the Danby Wiske estate. He was already very well liked by the king, and his influence was recognized by all who knew him. In 1617 he was knighted to become Sir George, and he was appointed as one of the king's favorite secretaries of state.

He had learned much during his years of minor investing with the Virginia Company, and he put every ounce of knowledge to use to make his fondest dream come true. In 1621

George helped found the colony of Avalon in Newfoundland. And shortly after Anne died in 1622, the king granted him an estate of 2,300 acres in County Longford, Ireland.

For years now, George had been hearing about the Americas, which had been discovered by the Spanish more than a century earlier. Stories of the untamed wilderness spread across England, along with tales of exotic natives, gold, and spices. It didn't matter that some of these claims were being made by men who had never been to the New World; the legends grew as certain brave souls who had crossed the Atlantic to see the land returned to England, armed with stories of land far as the eye could see. Towns, villages, and farms, the explorers insisted, could be created by the self-sustaining conditions of the land.

Newfoundland is the farthest east of Canada's 10 provinces, consisting of an island (Newfoundland) and the coast and interior of Labrador. It is also located at the most eastern section of the North American continent. Known for its different kinds of offshore sea life, Newfoundland ranks among the world's major fishing sites. St. John's is the province's capital city.

George helped found the colony of Avalon in Newfoundland, envisioning it as a place where religious freedom would reign. When George landed at the harbor, pictured here, there were no boats or houses, just unsettled land.

And so in 1623, Sir George, member of Parliament, principal secretary of state, asked the king for a grant of land in Newfoundland.

Because it was not safe for Catholics in England, George resigned as secretary of state. As a reward for his service to the Crown, in 1625 the king gave George the title of baron of Baltimore in the Kingdom of Ireland. George retired to his estate in Ireland and began planning a colony in the New World, where religious freedom would be the rule of the land. He went to Newfoundland twice, first in the summer of 1627, then in 1628. His new wife, Joan, accompanied him on his second visit, along with all but one of the children from his first marriage.

The Calverts remained less than a year before the climate and barren surroundings got to be too much for Joan. She packed up her belongings and headed south to Virginia, and early in 1629 George joined her there.

George decided to return to England, because he refused to swear allegiance to the Protestant

Crown and he hoped that he could persuade the king to decree that it was legal to practice Catholicism in the New World.

Despite his religious convictions, his friendship with King Charles I (who came to the throne in 1625) kept George's power fully intact. But even his close relationship with the king couldn't protect him from others. It wasn't safe for George to stay in his homeland.

Shortly after his arrival in England, George summoned his new wife and their young children home. During the months they were en route, he petitioned King Charles I for a grant of land south of the James River. The grant was awarded him in February of 1631. His joy over this success was short-lived, however,

To interest people in coming to Maryland, Lord Baltimore offered a variety of rewards, such as large land grants, government appointments, and noble titles. Anyone transporting enough people to receive a grant would have his tract designated a *manor*, complete with the right to hold court and other similar privileges. Lord Baltimore hoped this arrangement would help form a new nobility with powers and responsibilities like those established by the gentry in England, but the manorial system did not succeed in the colonies.

The colony of Maryland was named in honor of Queen Henrietta Maria, at the insistence of her husband, King Charles I.

for almost at the same time, George learned that the *St. Claude,* the ship that was carrying his family home, had been wrecked at sea soon after it became visible on the English horizon.

There was little left for him in his homeland. And so, in honor of Queen Mary, George wrote up a charter for lands north of Virginia. Once granted title to this territory, George would make his home there. He wanted to call his new colony Cresentia.

The king agreed to grant the land, as long as it would be named for his wife, Queen Henrietta Maria.

Queen Henrietta Maria (1609–1669) came from France but was not present at her marriage to the English King Charles I in 1625. She was only 15 at the time and her husband was 24. The queen was well regarded by her subjects at the beginning of her reign. However, her staunch belief in Roman Catholicism and favoritism toward the French soon led to anger among her subjects.

What was intended to be Maria's Land, or Marieland, soon became known as Maryland, one of the country's first colonies.

Sadly, George Calvert became ill and died in

Those who made the first voyage to Maryland were chosen for their particular skills. Some were farmers, others were carpenters and brick makers. Winter and summer clothes were necessary, as well as cannons, knives, and rifles for protection. Food aboard the ships had to be stored carefully so it would not spoil. Drinking water was stored in large casks, and great care was taken to protect the seeds of plants that would become food once the settlers reached the Maryland colony. When the 200-plus settlers arrived, they met the peaceable Piscataway Indians.

London on April 15, 1632, just two short months after the charter was granted, and before he saw the charter fully approved and sealed. His eldest son, Cecil Calvert, succeeded his father and inherited his titles, fortune, and lands. With these rights and privileges, Cecil saw to it that his father's wishes were carried out, and made sure that another charter was drafted. It went into effect on June 20, 1632.

Cecil sent his brothers, Leonard and George, on the first expedition to Maryland. They took two ships, the *Ark* and the *Dove,* and 200 men. The first settlers arrived on March 25, 1634, after passing through Barbados in the West Indies.

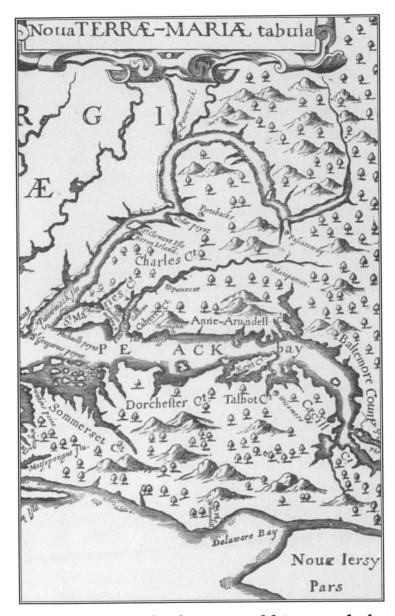

After George died, some of his sons led
the first expedition to Maryland. This
colonial map of "Maria's Land" dates
from a few decades later.

Today, Baltimore remains one of the country's most important harbors–the same harbor that inspired Francis Scott Key to write our national anthem.

Two thousand acres of land were promised to every man who agreed to transport five adult males as settlers to Maryland. This was known as a "headright." (As people began arriving in

Maryland, the acreage was reduced.) Land was acquired in three steps.

First, upon establishing a headright, a warrant was issued entitling the holder to lay out a stated number of acres anywhere within the province. Second, the surveyor prepared a certificate, identifying the boundaries of the survey and authorizing the holder to proceed to the third step, obtaining a patent that conveyed title to the land. Title was granted once the holder paid an annual tax to the landowner.

Named after Lord Baltimore, Baltimore is the largest city in the state of Maryland. It is located 35 miles northeast of the United States' capital city, Washington, D.C. The city boasts one of the country's most important ports. Francis Scott Key wrote the words to the song "The Star Spangled Banner," which became America's national anthem, while on a ship in Baltimore's harbor watching the British fire upon Fort McHenry during the War of 1812. The restored Inner Harbor district offers a wide selection of shops, restaurants, a science museum, and an aquarium.

St. Mary's, founded on March 27, 1634, was the first settlement in Maryland and the first seat of colonial government. Leonard Calvert established a governing body with an assembly of freemen and no religious restrictions on membership. This was a big step toward self-government.

Their father would have been proud to call Maryland his home, where he could have freely practiced his chosen religion.

GLOSSARY

archbishop chief bishop of a church district

armiger a knight's arms bearer

baron a nobleman; a man of great power in business or industry

charter document granting rights and privileges

convocation assembly

courier messenger

dispensation permission to stop or discontinue a rule

petition written request to person or people in authority

prominent important

retinue group of controllers

scholar well-educated person

theologian one who studies God or religion

tithe to donate a portion of one's wages—usually one-tenth—in
support of the church

treason betrayal of one's country

yeoman small landowner; naval officer who does clerical work

CHRONOLOGY

1580 In approximately this year, George Calvert is born in Yorkshire, England.

1594 George enters Oxford University.

1597 George earns his bachelor's degree.

1598 He enters law school at Lincoln's Inn, London.

1601 George leaves law school.

1603 George is appointed assistant secretary to Sir Robert Cecil, secretary of state.

1605 George marries Anne Mynne; he receives an honorary master's degree at Oxford.

1609 George is appointed clerk of the Signet.

1610 George is appointed clerk of the Privy Council.

1617 Knighted, he becomes Sir George.

1619 George becomes a principal secretary of state.

1621 George helps found the colony of Avalon in Newfoundland.

1622 Anne dies.

1623 George asks the king for additional land grants in Newfoundland.

1625 Publicly declaring himself a Catholic, George resigns his office as secretary of state.

1629 George goes to Virginia.

1631 George petitions King Charles I for land grants north of the James River.

1631 George loses his family in the shipwreck of the *St. Claude.*

1632 George Calvert dies in London on April 15; on June 20 the Maryland Charter is granted.

COLONIAL TIME LINE

1607 Jamestown, Virginia, is settled by the English.

1620 Pilgrims on the *Mayflower* land at Plymouth, Massachusetts.

1623 The Dutch settle New Netherland, the colony that later becomes New York.

1630 Massachusetts Bay Colony is started.

1634 Maryland is settled as a Roman Catholic colony. Later Maryland becomes a safe place for people with different religious beliefs.

1636 Roger Williams is thrown out of the Massachusetts Bay Colony. He settles Rhode Island, the first colony to give people freedom of religion.

1682 William Penn forms the colony of Pennsylvania.

1688 Pennsylvania Quakers make the first formal protest against slavery.

1692 Trials for witchcraft are held in Salem, Massachusetts.

1712 Slaves revolt in New York. Twenty-one blacks are killed as punishment.

1720 Major smallpox outbreak occurs in Boston. Cotton Mather and some doctors try a new treatment. Many people think the new treatment shouldn't be used.

1754 French and Indian War begins. It ends nine years later.

1761 Benjamin Banneker builds a wooden clock that keeps precise time.

1765 Britain passes the Stamp Act. Violent protests break out in the colonies. The Stamp Act is ended the next year.

1775 The battles of Lexington and Concord begin the American Revolution.

1776 Declaration of Independence is signed.

FURTHER READING

Fradlin, Dennis Brindele. *The Maryland Colony: The Thirteenth Colony.* Danbury, Conn.: Children's Press, 1990.

Foster, James W. *George Calvert: The Early Years.* Baltimore: Museum and Library of Maryland History, 1983.

Johnson, Walter J. *A Relation to Maryland: His Majesty's Charter to Lord Baltimore.* Self-published, 1976.

Marck, John T. *Maryland, the Seventh State: A History.* Baltimore: Maryland Historical Society, 1994.

The New Illustrated Columbia Encyclopedia. New York: Columbia University Press, 1995.

The Volume Library. Nashville, Tenn.: Southwest Company, 1995.

INDEX

INDEX

PICTURE CREDITS

ABOUT THE AUTHORS

A full-time freelancer for nearly 13 years, **LOREE LOUGH** has sold over 2,000 articles and dozens of short stories, novels for kids ages 8–12 (AMERICAN ADVENTURE), and 40 romances, including the award-winning *Pocketful of Love, Emma's Orphans, Kate Ties the Knot,* and *The Wedding Wish* (Heartsong presents). She has contributed to the best-selling anthologies *An Old Fashioned Christmas, Only You, I Do, Seasons of Love,* and *Winter Wishes* (Barbour Publishing). Her SUDDENLY series, published by Silhouette, has earned high marks from reviewers. Also writing as Aleesha Carter and Cara McCormack, Loree lives in Maryland with her husband and a cat named Mouser.

Senior Consulting Editor **ARTHUR M. SCHLESINGER, JR.** is the leading American historian of our time. He won the Pulitzer Prize for his book *The Age of Jackson* (1945) and again for *A Thousand Days* (1965). This chronicle of the Kennedy Administration also won a National Book Award. He has written many other books including a multi-volume series, *The Age of Roosevelt.* Professor Schlesinger is the Albert Schweitzer Professor of the Humanities at the City University of New York, and has been involved in several other Chelsea House projects, including the REVOLUTIONARY WAR LEADERS biographies on the most prominent figures of early American history.